Excerpts From My Heart

Order this book online at www.trafford.com
or email orders@trafford.com

Most Trafford titles are also available at major online book retailers.

Teacher Education Diploma; Child and Youth Counselor Diploma.

Printed in the United States of America.

ISBN: 978-1-4669-9086-9 (sc)
ISBN: 978-1-4669-9087-6 (e)

Trafford rev. 04/12/2013

 www.trafford.com

North America & international
toll-free: 1 888 232 4444 (USA & Canada)
phone: 250 383 6864 ♦ fax: 812 355 4082

❧ C o n t e n t s ❧

Motivation

Reflection

Making a Point

Contemplations

Tongue in Cheek

My Take

Foreword

I have come to the realization that if poetry does one thing, it is that it says a lot more about the poet than it does about anything else. At the end of the day it is about the poet's feelings, thoughts and perspectives. It is to a significant extent, about how he/she views his/her environment and his/her perception of how things unfold in his/her own consciousness. Therefore, when a poet shares his/her poems he/she is really sharing his/her deep feelings and thoughts. I am delighted to give you a glimpse into my ever evolving thought world.

This collection of poems reflects my experience and thoughts on various aspects of life. Poetry has given me a voice that I can use creatively to make a profound point or bring enlightenment. As an artistic form, poetry for me is not just about sweet sounding rhyming words and rhythmic flow, but a powerful medium for communication as well as an effective catharsis. In poetry the message supersedes the language as poetic license provides the latitude to break the exacting rules of grammar, where necessary.

However useful you find these poems to be it must be credited to family and encouraging friends who have directly and indirectly supported my continuous development of poetic expressions. Thanks to my wife TracyAnn and daughter Lavanya for supporting my efforts and tolerating my recitals even at inappropriate times. My oldest sister Deberan is responsible for my initial love for reading, and hence my first steps into the land of creative imagination as well as my younger sister Flavia, who shares my love for poetic expressions and appreciation for great writing.

I dedicate this collection of poems to my deceased grandmother who raised me from I was three months old. Any and every achievement that I attain must be credited to her purposeful and tireless efforts to raise me well. She succeeded at it and for that I am eternally grateful.

Fearfully and Wonderfully Man

Fearfully and wonderfully I was made man

Not a cosmic accident but a purposeful plan

Each morning in the sunrise I see more than what shines

I know I am presented a gift most sublime

My ears behold the chirping of the birds in the tree

And I know inside they were made to sing for me

I may not have the fortune of monetary wealth

But I'm blessed and highly favoured with beautiful health

I can think and make decisions and express just how I feel

I can posit my opinions and affix to them my seal

I can critique or compliment the things that I behold

I can sing aloud melody or hum a tune in my soul

I do not have to be the sweetest cookie in the jar

But someone somewhere thinks I am far above the stars

I may not have the gift of gab or speech of eloquence

But I have moved from average valley to the mount of excellence

I am not a subject of comparison I am just uniquely me

I am one leaf, one branch, one stem, on the diverse human tree

Come on brothers and sisters don't be a self-defeating drag

Inside you is that gift un-wrapped, that you thought you never had

Step into the ring; take the bull by its horn

Put your feet on troubled waters; rise up high above the storm

You were not made for the day; the day was made for you

You can make it what you want, and tell it what to do

In the fluttering of the birds wings and the rustling of the leaves

Someone made it for your pleasure, hoping you would be pleased

Tragic is any moment to spurn this grand design

Such a masterpiece of workmanship; a beautiful mind

Roll back the curtain; in the spotlight take your stand

Be all that it means to be fearfully and wonderfully man

Man Up!

Stand up; step up and man up!
Don't weep; don't whimper; don't waffle
Don't grumble, don't gripe; don't grabble
Lose the long list of don'ts
Take your mind off the won'ts
Then stand up; step up and man up!

Stand up; step up and man up!
Dont quibble! Don't quiver! Dont quit!
Dont deny! Dont decline! Dont demit!
Play the game and take the blame.
Learn your lessons and bear your shame.
Then stand up; step up and man up!

Stand up; step up and man up!
Don't grieve! Don't growl! Don't grovel!
Don't hide! Don't hinder! Don't haggle!
Take your licks and learn new tricks.
Use your words, not stones and sticks.
Then stand up; step up and man up!

Stand up; step up and man up!
Don't tarry! Don't tumble! Don't twaddle!
Don't loaf! Don't loot! Don't litter!
Take your loss and suck it up.
Drink from the boiling cup.
Then stand up; step up and man up!

Stand up; step up and man up!
Don't guess! Don't gossip! Don't giggle!
Don't plea! Don't protest; Don't prattle!
Put your shoulder to the wheel
Bend your strong back of steel
Then stand up; step up and man up!

Just Be

Why don't you be the change you wish to see
The peace you crave; the justice you seek
The oneness you hope for; the unity you preach,
Why don't you just be

Why don't you be the change you wish to see
Be the man you wish that every man would be
Be upright and noble, affirm your humanity
Stake your claim and never shun responsibility
Take the road less travelled; let the change begin with you
Why don't you just be

Why don't you be the change you wish to see
Be the woman that you wish every woman would be
One whose beauty transcends the latest bling
One whose identity is not tied to possession or position
But in the reality of being a child of the KING
Why don't you just be

Why don't you be the change you wish to see
Why curse the darkness when you can be the light
Why cave in and compromise when you can put up a fight
Be the man! Take a stand! Be the one
Don't quiver, just deliver; be strong
And be the change you wish to see

Be Assertive

Be assertive and speak your piece
Your views are by no means the least
Speak your mind if you're impressed
Yours is as important as the rest
Speak out clearly your agreements
Posit them firmly with much confidence
Equally be bold when you disagree
Make your expressions honest and free
The rights of others you must always respect
But never feel fettered when you need to project
Be purposeful in all deliberations
And always be ready to make decisions
Assert your stance and be direct
Don't falter or waver to the right or the left

Becoming

Crude and cantankerous with millions of faults

Yet progressively better than I was in the past

You say as a believer I should walk in the way

I acknowledge my failings that's why I pray

You decry my opinions and belittle my thoughts

But I'm forever thanking God for His gift on the cross

I agree I'm a snub, weird and egocentric

On my knees I do tarry, praying hard about it

You may say I am not perfect and unworthy of praise

But one thing is certain, we're all sinners saved by grace

Tell me I am unworthy; tell me I'm full of it

It's not by power or by might, but by His Spirit

You can be my judge and jury; sweep your dirt under the rug

A certain day is coming when we all shall face the judge

Point your finger when I slip; sneer and jeer when I slide

I am better than I use to be; God will be my guide

Enjoy pointing to my history; all my failings please explore

I have long served notice; I don't live there anymore

Turn up the music, and play the judgment song

You just can't resist it, Mr and Mrs Historian

Watch me as I stumble and rise up again

You will never see me as I am but as I had been

Gather all the mud; paint me with your slime

You are sitting in a valley from which I long climbed

Born to Be Me

I was not born to call, but to be called on
I was not born to be boastful, but to be helpful
I was not born to be slavishly led, but to follow and lead
I was not born to be driven, but to drive
I was not born to be served, but to be of service
I was not born to be defeated but to compete and succeed
I was not born to be a taker, but to be conscientious giver
I was not born to be poor but to prosper
I was not born to dwell in the cellar of mediocrity
But to strive on the summit of excellence
I was not born to be stopped by obstacles
But to convert them into miracles
I will not be bought, I am here to buy
I will be who I am becoming
And who I am becoming will be me
I will sing to their tune
But it is my song I'll be singing at noon
I will compare myself
But I will be that comparison
I will compete with others
But I will be my fiercest competition
I will be criticized,
But I am my harshest critic
I will be cheered on,
But I will be my biggest cheerleader
I will not relent, I will persist
I will live and not just merely exist
I will laugh more than I cry
I will walk until I can't, and then I will fly
Under His leadership I will navigate this ship called me
I will ride the waves of this unpredictable and pernicious sea
And when on the mountain of achievement I stand
I will still be reaching down with a helping hand

The Shadow of Doubt

I shook off the stifling shadow of doubt
That blocked me whenever I try to break out
Sapping the creative juice I possess
Pushing me off the cliff of distress
Breaking the back of my self-confidence
Crushing my hopes to achieve excellence
Telling me everyone is better than me
And that I have been all I ever will be
So I revved up my engine of self belief
Jumped over the hurdles of self-pity and grief
Opened the gate that leads to success
Relinquished the better and grabbed hold of the best
I silenced the doubters and confounded my foes
Launched brutal attacks with devastating blows
Scattered seeds of confusion in the enemy's camp
Jabbing and punching like a heavy weight champ
Employed shock and awe to give them the jolt
Moving at speeds much faster than Bolt
Installed firewalls to safely protect
From spies and voyeurs who like to inspect
So friends I counsel you heed this advice
From the stale bread of doubt don't eat a slice
Don't ever waver to believe in yourself
Examine options and choose from the shelf
What you shall be is all in your grasp
So Let doubt be a joke at which you just laugh

Ring the Bells

Ring the bells of freedom; ring them on yonder hills
Let them permeate the atmosphere with liberating chills
Let them loose your tangled feet to dance a happy song
Share the news with your friends inviting them along
Let the bells of freedom be heard in every speech
Let them stir your actions, not just what you preach

Ring the bells of tolerance; embrace those unlike you
We don't have to achieve sameness to be genuinely true
We may not eat the same food or share artistic taste
Still don't put those bells away, in any undue haste
Share it with the stranger you meet on the street
Sway neatly with the melodies so soulful and sweet

Ring the bells of unity; let them truly resonate
Let them be the voice of love that conquers bitter hate
Let them dull the edge of differences; harness shared goals
Let them lift wilting spirits and revive dormant souls
Erase those cruel lines that tangle and divide
Let's build a wall of unity and all gather on one side

Ring those bells of happiness so rapturous and loud
Use them like a magic wand to dispel sadness cloud
Ring them in the darkness; ring them in the light
Ring them when the creepy snake comes out to crawl at nights
Ring them when doubt sets in and fear takes a hold
Ring them with such majesty; be fearlessly bold

HOPE

Hang high your hope let it blow in the air
Tie it like a ribbon in a baby girl's hair
Hoist high your hope on the flag pole of life
Let it ever rise above the heartaches and strife
Lift up your hope let it dictate your course
Make it your ally, such a dynamic force
Point your hope upward, like a rocket off to space
When you falter in the trenches, let it quicken your pace
Adorn your hope like a blushing bride
Just never let it stray from your side
Hold it and squeeze it close to your heart
Pledge you and her never will part
Hug close your hope, without it you're dead
It's the root of prosperity that grows in your head
So dream more, hope much and reach your very best
Hope springs eternal from the human breast

Day Break

What countless blessings that comes
with day break
My heart rejoices with decisions to
make
Another rough night is over
Taking with it life's frustrated past
Now I have beauty like a clover
Because daybreak has come at last
The sun bursts the pregnant horizon
Its piercing rays cuts the dark
The birds sing sweetly in unison
And it melts my grateful heart

Life's deck of cards has dealt me
another hand to play
And I intend to use it like it's my very
last day
Thank God I am alive and well
Today I must make progress
I have good reasons to excel
Because I am truly blessed
I may not see tomorrow's sun
That's beyond my control
But today is a race that I must run
With my mind, body and soul

Hold On

When the pain of life weakens your grip
When numbness pervades your finger tips
When the hands of stress choke your neck
When your blistered, tired back hits the deck
When it feels like you are all alone
When no one bothers to call your phone
Hold on, don't let go!

When your feet are tied right and left
When you are broke and deep in debt
When your lover breaks your heart
When you lose before you start
When your sun refuse to shine
When problems weigh on your mind
Hold on, don't let go!

When your best friend turn on you
When you don't know what to do
When your pay falls short of your bills
When everything seems to be uphill
When your world comes crashing in
When you don't know where to begin
Hold on, don't let go!

Hold on to who you really are
Hold on if you alone must wage the war
Hold on if only you believe your dreams
Hold on when going fast downstream
Hold on when your faith is shaken
Hold on when you're heavy laden
Hold on! Hold on! Hold on!

The Will

The ability to act and the will to do
Are vital tools to make a better you
Countless persons have failed to attain
Not because they did not have a brain
They possessed the ability and skill
But they just did not possess the will

Many geniuses have been born
But the robe of success from them was torn
They were adept in concept formation
But fell sterilely impotent in implementation

Many men know how to please
When to be serious and how to tease
They can talk you through a transaction
But fail to deliver any action

Many preachers know what to say
Preach the best of sermons and love to pray
They expound biblical exegesis with clarity
But never extend a hand in charity

Many great doctors can fix your health
Explain a condition and say why you belch
Write a prescription for the perfect pill
While their health slip away downhill

Many politicians make promises
Effectively communicate their messages
Only to find after an election
They are woefully missing in action

Until we combine ability and will
The road of progress will be uphill
When we conceive what we should do
We should have the will to see it through

Fragile

Oh life how flimsy and fragile thou art

You mark us with death right from the start

Yet how fulfilling in so many ways

How careful we should be to number our days

Friends that we make, secrets we keep

Soon to be parted at the end of the street

Fun things we do, memories we cherish

In the throb of a heartbeat, fatally perish

The sweet taste of victories, emotions we feel

Yet pain often shakes our platform of steel

From the cradle to the graveyard

A grim but sobering fact

Along the way let's play hard

No regrets looking back

The evanescent nature of youthful bloom

Melts like a candle, gone too soon

Each moment is precious; enjoy what you do

Pilgrims in paradise, just passing through . . . .

Death

Oh death you sound so final as an enemy of man

Your nature is brutal as you ravage the land

You are not a friend but a certain foe

When my number plays only you will know

But I do not fear as I know from where you came

You are just a door to walk through, when eternal life I claim

I won't let you cause me stress; I understand your role

If I live my life for Jesus you will never get my soul

When you stop by for me, it will just be for a while

Because I'll awake to meet the Redeemer of my life

Meet You In My Dreams Mama!

When the waves of nostalgia wash me ashore

On the refuging wings of my dream I soar

I wander the turbid streets of memories alone

Recall peals of laughter that once lit our home

No more chances of sharing between me and you

But I treasure the many things you taught me to do

Re-learning the lessons that you once taught

Drink from the stream that flows from your heart

Eating the food you made with your hands

Watching you implementing your plans

From your silent prayers come echoes of pleas

Guide for my voyage on life troubled seas

I still hear the stories you told me at nights

Of past days of hardships and dwindling lights

Of childhood adventures and perilous times

Of failures, successes, of lemons and limes

But then there were things that were not said

The things we acknowledged as you tucked me in bed

The unspoken love that lit up your eyes

The depth of your care that was heard in your sighs

The distress and worry when I was not well

The tales that only your great heart could tell

The assurance that those times when I did not pray

The top of your prayer list is where I would stay

But now that you have ceased to be

I have one less angel to pray for me

And when I awake from the shadows of dream

I drown in a tearful and sorrowful stream

Life Is

Life can be a bed of roses if you live it as you should

Not elevating the negative over the noble and the good

It can be just as easy as rolling down the hill

Or as stressful as having no funds to pay the bill

Life is tending to the flowers and watering the seeds

Helping out the neighbours raking up the leaves

Life is taking time to say, "Sir, how do you do?"

And actually listen to what he has to say to you

Life is laying in the grass and staring at the sky

Oblivious to all else that's hastily passing by

Life is chasing after butterflies and playing in the rain

Telling jokes with your friends; call each other funny names

Life is walking down a quiet street singing a happy song

And nodding your approval to those who care to sing along

Life is reaping your tomatoes to share with your friends

Entertaining strangers and inviting them again

Life is sharing your last dime with those in dire need

Eating a sumptuous fruit, then promptly plants the seed

Life is living in the moment and really makes it counts

Being careful of the words proceeding from your mouth

Life is bursting with laughter at no one's expense

Trading in bureaucracy for a dose of common sense

Life is calling up your foe to tell him he's forgiven

Caring for the homeless and visit those in prison

Life is being there for someone, nudging them ahead

Thanking all your friends now and not when they are dead

Life is spending time with your daughter and playing with your son

Finding purpose in your pursuits and passion in your fun

Life is eating with your bare hands in a world of knife and fork

Accepting of who people are with their freckles and warts

Life is lynching legalism and exalting liberty

Embracing individualism and preach prosperity.

Life, is knowing that it is a gift, given only once

It pays therefore to live it well; you never get a second chance

Bovrell G. Simpson

P e a c e

When peace like a river attends your way

Don't let it slip by invite her to stay

Make it be your soul-mate, your very special friend

It will come to your rescue when misfortune does you in

Wrap peace around your anger when someone earns your wrath

Pour it all over your temper; it is good for the heart

Let peace hold your tongue when you're pushed to spill the beans

Bask in it's of calmness, so pleasant and serene

Make peace be your restraint, when you're forced to punch him out,

When you're angered by filthy words spewing from his mouth

Speak peace because it's healthy; speak peace because it's right

Preach peace in the darkness, preach peace in the light

When you are peaceful the whole world can tell

You can sing hallelujah! With my soul it is well

Slow Down

When was the last time you paused life's speeding wheel

Reminisce with a friend and share just how you feel

Old Tom down the road hasn't seen you in a while

Been so long since your face showed a genuine smile

Grandma expressed her longing to see your face

The time is ripe to contemplate slowing down the pace

Slow down the rush and smell the fresh bloomed roses

Note the beauty of those around you and the smiles upon their faces

Someone longs with desperation for a minute of your time

Not everything in life should be pegged to a dime

De-construct the equation that puts things above people

Where went the good old days when things were good and simple

Do we stop to watch the sun glides across the sky

Be that big strong shoulder for those who want to cry

Where in town does the stranger sit to ponder for a while

Can we find our way to the village that raised the child

Not because a town has a cemetery in the square

Gives us cause for a mad rush to take a spot in there

Slow down, smell the coffee, even take a sip or two

If you must rush, then let this be said of you

He loved people much more than wealth and fame

All good, noble and worthy things bore his name

She lived life at its fullest short-changing no one

Courageous in goodwill; had a love so true and strong

From the factory to the scrap heap, cars speeding by

Once new and squeaky, now junk piled high

Life is not a mad rush from the cradle to the grave

We will all get there one day, from the timid to the brave

So count the blessings of friendship and the value of time

Exchange nonessentials for things transcendently sublime

Looking Back

Beholding my foot prints on life's troubled shore

Pondering if I could have done any more

Pausing to rest in retrospect's shade

Scrutinizing the list of decisions I've made

If fate has decided the best I can be

Then I'm not the ruler of my own destiny

Possessing no power over time's master clock

Wonder how useful it is looking back

There is no way back to undo what's done

A bullet does not return to a smoking gun

A word once spoken remains expressed

And life has its share of painful regrets

Seems a man has to play the hand he is dealt

Pull up his pants and fasten his belt

Some things never change no matter the source

Seems like onward and forward is the only recourse

Life is a Gift

To see your life as a gift
And your skills the tools
To feel your duty is to uplift
Puts you way above all fools

To have a mind to care
A heart to empathize
To love away clouds of fear
Is a most treasured prize

To feel desire deep inside
To serve and not be served
To exhibit humble pride
Takes more than sheer nerve

To decay on life's scrap heap
To sit and never try
Is to see your life as cheap
Slowly waste away and die

You can see life as a duty
Rated high above a chore
It's an absolute beauty
When you care for the poor

Today

A plant burst through the ground today
To greet the morning sun
It took its first step on the way
To a task that must be done
It fluttered in the morning breeze
And soaked up oxygen
A replacement for fallen leaves
Whose time came to an end

❖

A special child was born today
A sweet little girl
Though she had no words to say
She was glad to see the world
Grief and loss, pain and shame
Awaits her innocence
Love and laughter she will claim
To enrich her experience

❖

A car came of the assembly line
Today somewhere out there
It looks so beautiful and fine
With cool gadgets and flare
It will decrease in value
Despite the price you'll pay
What they will fail to tell you
Is that it's heading for decay

Today a new idea was born
That someday might change the world
What started as a quiet storm
Will soon explosively unfurl
It might affect the way you think
Or the way you move
It could push us all to the brink
Or your life improves

Two hearts fell in love today
Now they beat as one
They pass the time in happy play
Two lovers that belong
As they walk along and kiss
The world for them stands still
This sweet dream of happy bliss
Might hold for them endless thrill

We Don't Have To Agree

I TELL YOU WHAT I KNOW AND I MAY NOT BE RIGHT

I SHOW YOU WHAT I SEE AND IT MIGHT ELUDE YOUR SIGHT

I HAVE MY OWN OPINIONS, YOU MAY NOT AGREE WITH THEM

THE WAY I WEAR MY HAIR MIGHT BE YOUR BIGGEST PROBLEM

YOU MAY NOT LIKE THE WAY THAT I WALK ACROSS THE STREET

OR SHARE THE SAME TASTE OF THE FOOD THAT I EAT

WE MAY AT SOME POINT HAVE TO GO OUR SEPARATE WAYS

AND COULD UNITE AT SOME POINT FOR MANY BETTER DAYS

BUT WE DON'T HAVE TO AGREE

WE DON'T HAVE TO SHARE THE SAME SEAT ON THE BENCH

AND I AM NOT PERTURBED BY YOUR INDEPENDENCE

WE CAN CLIMB THE STAIRS TOGETHER OR WALK A MILE ALONE

YOU CAN TEXT ME IF YOU WANT, OR TELL ME ON THE PHONE

WE DO NOT HAVE TO CHEER FOR THE SAME SPORTS TEAM

AND I MAY LAUGH AND GIGGLE WHILE YOU JUST WANT TO

SCREAM

BUT WE DON'T HAVE TO AGREE

IT'S OK TO THINK I'M HERE BY SOME DIVINE PLAN

AND YOU CAN CREDIT YOUR EXISTENCE TO EVOLUTION

WE DO NOT HAVE AGREE ON THE CHICKEN OR THE EGG

OR EVEN SHARE THE SAME VIEW ON THE STATE OF THE DEAD

IT'S OKAY TO BE WRONG; WE CANNOT ALL BE RIGHT

YOU HAVE THE RIGHT TO BE WRONG AND FOR THAT I WILL

FIGHT

BUT WE DON'T HAVE TO AGREE

WE CAN CREATE A COMMUNITY OF TOLERANCE AND LIBERTY

WE CAN CELEBRATE THE VALUE OF OUR RICH DIVERSITY

WE CAN CHANGE A HEART WITHOUT LOSING A FRIEND

WE CAN BUILD A ROAD TO FRIENDSHIP THAT NEVER HAS AN

END

WE CAN LOVE A NEIGHBOUR JUST BECAUSE IT'S RIGHT TO DO

I CAN WEAR MY SLIPPERS AND YOU CAN WEAR SHOES

BUT WE DON'T HAVE TO AGREE

You Deserve It

When you have gone an inch too far
When you have openly declared war
When you have crossed one line too many
When you've declared yourself an enemy
When you have dug one grave too few
And think the world revolves around you
You deserve it; you deserve what's coming to you

When the smile you forced is not real
And you rush to condemn with zeal
When the course you pursue is not right
And you are quick to start up a fight
When you cheat and lie to get even
And you hate and despise without reason
You deserve it; you deserve what's coming to you

❖

WHEN YOU TWIST AND MANGLE THE TRUTH

WHEN REVENGE CHARACTERIZE YOUR PURSUIT

WHEN YOU MASK AND EMBELLISH THE WORD

AND BEHAVE LIKE A SPIRITUAL NERD

WHEN YOU SLIP AND FALL ON YOUR SWORD

I WILL HELP YOU TO GET BACK ON BOARD

THOUGH YOU DESERVE IT

I'LL SHOW GRACE AND MERCY TO YOU

BUT YOU DESERVE IT; YOU DESERVE WHAT'S COMING TO YOU

ALL IN ITS TIME

IN ITS TIME THINGS ONCE LONGED FOR WILL UNFOLD

IN ITS TIME THINGS ONCE KEPT SECRET WILL BE TOLD

THE WALLS ONCE STRONG WILL AT LAST TUMBLE

THE ROCK THOUGH SOLID WILL ALSO CRUMBLE

THE ARCHITECT OF EVIL WILL MEET HIS DEMISE

THE MAN PLAGUED WITH ERRORS WILL LEARN TO BE WISE

AND AS MANY WILL RISE UP AND MANY WILL FALL

FIERCE CHALLENGES WILL DRIVE US SOMETIMES TO THE WALL

WE WILL SEEK FOR A BREAK AND SEE NONE IN SIGHT

WE WILL FIGHT GREAT BATTLES IN THE DARKEST OF NIGHT

EN-ROUTE ON THIS JOURNEY WE SEARCH FOR A SIGN

BUT THINGS SEEM TO HAPPEN ALL IN ITS TIME

ALL IN ITS TIME TEARS LONG SHED WILL BE WIPED AWAY

DEBTS LONG OWED WILL INDEED BE PAID

JUSTICE LONG DUE WILL FINALLY BE SERVED

WE WON'T LONG REMAIN IN THE LEARNING CURVE

THE CONSTANCY OF CHANGE MUST BE ETCHED IN OUR MINDS

DON'T FORGET THAT THINGS HAPPEN ALL IN ITS TIME

❖

ALL IN ITS TIME MEMORIES SO DEAR WILL FADE AWAY

THAT LONG DREADFUL NIGHT WILL TURN INTO DAY

THE HELPLESS CHILD WILL GROW TO BE STRONG

THE WINDING TRAIL WON'T SEEM ALL THAT LONG

SOMETIMES WE FEEL THAT THINGS SHOULD MOVE FASTER

ONE FACT REMAINS CERTAIN; TIME IS THE MASTER

EVERY NOW AND THEN

EVERY NOW AND THEN SOMETHING
HAPPENS TO BRING US BACK TO
EARTH
CONCEALED SKELETON IN CLOSETS
SOON SHOW UP AT OUR
DOORSTEPS
THE NOBLE DEEDS WE PUSH ASIDE
COME RIDING HIGH ON THE
EVENING TIDE
THE THINGS FOR WHICH WE DID
NOT CARE
GREET US SQUARELY WITH A STARE
THOSE FOR WHOM WE COULD
CARE LESS
BECOME OUR SHIELD AND PLACE
OF REST
THE THINGS YOU SWORE YOU'D
NEVER DO
BECOME SO MUCH A PART OF YOU

❖

EVERY NOW AND THEN SOMETHING

HAPPENS, TO SHOW WE ARE NOT
PERFECT
THINGS UNRAVEL, FALL APART
SHATTERED DREAMS AND BROKEN
HEARTS
THOSE WE MOCK, DESPISE, AND
DERIDE
BECOME VALIANT ALLIES BY OUR
SIDE
THINGS WE CHERISHINGLY REFUSE
TO SHARE
SOON BECOME OUR WORST
NIGHTMARE
THE THING FOR WHICH WE HURT
AND MAIM
SOON WILL YIELD MUCH SHAME
AND PAIN
THE MOUNTAINS WE REFUSE TO
CLIMB
LEAVE LINGERING REGRETS IN OUR
MINDS

❖

EVERY NOW AND THEN
SOMETHING HAPPENS, THAT
SHAKES OUR GROUND OF STEEL
THE FRIEND YOU THOUGHT YOU'D

NEVER LOSE

LEAVE YOU SHAKING IN YOUR

SHOES

THE WELL YOU THOUGHT WOULD

NOT RUN DRY

IS SOON DEPLETED WHEN THE

STAKES ARE HIGH

THE THINGS ON WHICH YOU SO

DEPEND

AS SURE AS A SUNRISE WILL COME

TO AN END

THE CAUSE, FOR WHICH YOU

STAND AND FIGHT

WILL OFTEN CAUSE YOU SLEEPLESS

NIGHTS

THE STAKE YOU CLAIM THAT

BROUGHT YOU FAME

SOME DAYS JUST BRING YOU PAIN

AND SHAME

❖

EVERY NOW AND THEN

SOMETHING HAPPENS, TO SHOW

WHO WE ARE

THOSE ALONG JUST FOR THE RIDE

NEVER MOUNT THE RISING TIDE

THOSE WHOSE FEET ARE OFF THE

GROUND

NEVER STAND WHEN THE CHIPS

ARE DOWN

THOSE NOT POSSESSING GOOD

ATTITUDE

WILL NEVER GAIN GREAT ALTITUDE

THOSE WHO FIGHT AND RUN

AWAY

WILL LIVE TO FIGHT ANOTHER DAY

THOSE REFUSED TO STAND LIKE A

BRAVE

SLEEP HOPELESSLY IN SHALLOW

GRAVES

WE DON'T KNOW HOW; WE DON'T

KNOW WHEN

BUT THINGS DO HAPPEN NOW

AND THEN

Here Today

LIKE PLANTS AT SOME POINT WE FADE AWAY
TODAY'S GREEN GRASS AND TOMORROW'S DRIED HAY
PLANTED, WATERED, AND NOURISHED TO GROW
REAPED AND STORED OR COVERED IN SNOW

TODAY'S NEW CAR IS ON TOMORROW'S JUNK HEAP
MATTERS NOT HOW EXPENSIVE OR HOW CHEAP
THE CRADLE TO GRAVEYARD AS SURE AS FATE
ALL HEADING FOR DECAY HOWEVER SOON OR LATE

TODAY'S NEW BABY SOON TO BE GROWN
STANDING IN THE CRIB SITTING ON A THRONE
FROM THE PEWS OF THE CHURCH TO THE FUNERAL HOME
FROZEN IN TIME IN A DARK AND HOLLOW DOME

TODAY'S BRIGHT SMILE, TOMORROW'S PAINFUL FROWN

THAT THIN LINE BETWEEN THE CLERGY AND A CLOWN

FROM A JOLLY GOOD FELLOW TO A SCOLDING CHILD

HEADING TO THE SAME PLACE, TAME AND WILD

TODAY'S STUMBLING BLOCK; TOMORROW'S STEPPING STONE

THE BATTLES THAT WE MUST FIGHT, OFTEN ALONE

LIVING FOR TODAY; FIGHTING FOR TOMORROW'S SUN

STRUTTING MY BRAVADO EVEN WHEN I WANT TO RUN

Lonely Streets of Mud

KNOCKED FACE DOWN ON THE MUDDY STREETS OF MY MIND

CAN'T SEE THROUGH THE MUCK THAT'S MAKING ME BLIND

FOOTSTEPS RETREATING INTO DISTANT SHADOWS

I STRUGGLE ALONE IN THE MUD THAT I WALLOW

THE WEIGHT OF LIFE CARES PRESSING ME DOWN

PUNCHING AND POUNDING ME INTO THE GROUND

TEASING AND TAUNTING AS I STUMBLE AND SLIP

TAKING ANOTHER OF THEIR KICKS ON MY LIPS

THE SONG OF HOSANNA RECEDES IN THE PAST

CRUCIFIXION DAY HAS QUICKLY COME AT LAST

NO FRIENDS OR FANS TO PULL A BROTHER UP

ALONE AND ISOLATED TO DRINK THE BITTER CUP

SOME THINGS IN LIFE A MAN MUST DO ALONE

DESPITE THOUSANDS OF CONTACTS ON HIS CELL PHONE

HE MUST BEAR THE PAIN OF LIFE'S MANY TESTS

TURNING BITTER GRAPES INTO WINE OF BETTER-NESS

PROVING FIRST TO HIM-SELF OF WHAT HE IS MADE

BEFORE LEADING OTHERS ON THE GRAND OLD PARADE

THE MUD OF THE STREET WILL DRY AND TURN TO DUST

AND THE WIND OF TIME WILL BLOW AWAY THE CRUST

THE LIGHTS WILL RETURN AND THEN YOU WILL SEE

HOW FRIENDLY YOUR FRIENDS AND FANS CAN BE

DEEDS

NO ONE SEEMED TO NOTICE WHEN HE QUIETLY LEFT THE STAGE

SOME WERE HAPPY AT HIS EXIT; SOME WERE SIMPLY DISENGAGED

HIS TIME IN THE SPOTLIGHT BARELY EVER CAUSED A STIR

BUT HE SURELY RECEIVED HIS FAIR AMOUNT OF LESS THAN

FRIENDLY STARES

HIS WORDS DID NOT INSPIRE, UPLIFT OR EDIFY

HOPES ABOUNDED AT HIS ENTRY, MOVING SOME TO PROPHESY

NOTHING SPOKEN WAS NOTEWORTHY, TO EVOKE GREAT APPLAUSE

NO EFFORT TO ATTACH HIMSELF TO A SINGLE WORTHY CAUSE

LIFE TO HIM WAS FOR LIVING; NO THOUGHT FOR FRIENDS

HE WAS THE ALL; THE ONLY MEANS AND THE NARROW ENDS

NO ONE WAS ENLIGHTENED BY THE KNOWLEDGE HE POSSESSED

NOW HE HAS PLAYED HIS LAST NOTE, AND AT LAST LAID TO REST

❖

WHO WILL SING HIS MEMORIES; WHAT WILL BE HIS EPITAPH

WHO WILL EULOGIZE HIM; WHO CAN TRACK HIS TRACE-LESS PATH

WILL WE PONDER IF HE TRULY LIVED, OR MERELY JUST EXIST

CAN ONE UNDO LIFE'S MISSTEPS, LOOKING UP FROM SIX FOOT SIX

❖

SEEMS THE ONLY WAY DO IT RIGHT, IS DOING IT RIGHT, AND NOW

WHILE THE HANDS ARE STILL STURDY AND THE HEAD IS YET TO BOW

WHILE THE EYES ARE STILL BRIGHT AND THE DAY BEGINS AT DAWN

IT IS FAR TOO LATE TO SCATTER ROSES, AFTER ONE IS GONE

WALK IN MY SHOES

TAKE A WALK WITH ME TO THE TOP OF MY HILL

PUT ON MY SHOES AND WEAR IT FOR A SPELL

IT'S WORN AND WILL NOT KEEP OUT THE CHILL

BUT THIS IS MY WORLD AND MOST TIMES IT IS HELL

LET US EXCHANGE CULTURE AND ETHNICITY

EXPERIENCE HOW THE WORLD TREATS ME

FEEL WHAT IT MEANS TO BE YOUNG, POOR AND BLACK

GET USE TO BEING ALWAYS PUSHED TO THE BACK

FEEL THE HARDSHIPS THAT I HAVE OVERCOME

AND BEAR IT IN MIND THE NEXT TIME YOU POKE FUN

DON'T COMPLAIN MY FRIEND, THIS IS THE OTHER HALF

THE COW THAT YOU SEE TODAY GREW FROM A CALF

EACH OF US HAS A UNIQUE PERSPECTIVE

AND NOT EVERYONE CAN AFFORD HOW YOU LIVE

NO DON'T QUIT YET, FOLLOW ME TO SCHOOL

SIT IN MY CLASS AND BE TREATED LIKE A FOOL

YES, I CAN SEE WHY YOU WANT TO STOP

YOU'RE AFRAID TO ALWAYS BE STOPPED BY A COP

LET'S EXCHANGE CHILDHOOD EXPERIENCE

BECOME THE POOR CHILD OF MY PARENTS

WALK BAREFOOT TO SCHOOL COME RAIN OR SHINE

TAKE LICKS ON YOUR RUMP FOR NOT SHOWING UP ON TIME

TASTE HOW IT FEELS TO ALWAYS LOSE

WALK THE ROCKY PATHS WITHOUT ANY SHOES

CLIMB UP MY HILL AND GET USE TO THE DRUDGE

DON'T FORGET IT THE NEXT TIME YOU THINK TO BE MY JUDGE

Chains of Circumstances

AWAKEN THIS MORNING WITH CHAINS ON MY FEET

CHAINS OF DISTRESS AND IMPENDING DEFEAT

CHAINS OF HARDSHIPS AND EXTREME SCARCITY

CHAINS OF CHAOS AND TRIBAL DISUNITY

CHAINS OF CLASSISM AND DISPARITY

CHAINS OF INJUSTICE AND INEQUALITY

LYING FACE DOWN IN A MESS OF DEFICIT

TRYING SO HARD TO WORK MY BUDGET

FIERCELY PURSUED BY THE MONSTER OF CRIME

LANGUISHING BENEATH THE POVERTY LINE

ESCAPED ANOTHER AMBUSH LATE LAST NIGHT

YET NOTHING SEEMS TO APPEASE MY PLIGHT

THE LANDLORD'S RAGE HAS BECOME A CYCLONE

JUST A MATTER OF TIME AND I'LL HAVE NO HOME

THE PREACHER IS BUSY WITH THE WORD TO SPREAD

AND NO ONE HAS TIME FOR SHARING THE BREAD

MY NEIGHBOUR STRUGGLES WITH CHAINS OF HIS OWN

LAST NIGHT HE WAS FIGHTING HIS DOG FOR A BONE

WHAT IS IMMERGING IS PATENTLY CLEAR

LIFE HAS HARDSHIPS AND IS NOT FAIR

A MAN IS ONLY FREE WHEN HE DREAMS

THERE HE CAN DO WHATEVER HE DEEMS

THERE HE STANDS TALL WITHOUT ANY CHAINS

HE SINGS WITH THE BIRDS AND PLAYS IN THE RAIN

BEAUTY IS FOREVER!

WHEN THE RADIANT JUICE OF YOUTH DRIES UP

AND YOU'VE SUP THE LAST DROP FROM BEAUTY'S CUP

WHEN IN THE MIRROR YOU LONGINGLY PLEA

FOR DAYS WHEN YOU WERE GLOWING WITH GLEE

WHEN THE WAR OF THE BULGE YOU HOPELESSLY FIGHT

WHEN RETROSPECTIVELY YOU REMINISCE AT NIGHTS

NO NEED TO DESPAIR, JUST GO WITH THE FLOW

YOU ARE LEARNING LESSONS YOUR PARENTS LONG KNOW

THE BOOK OF YOUR LIFE HAS A MUCH BETTER CHAPTER

LIFE'S PRIMARY TASK IS TO ADORN YOUR CHARACTER

TRUE BEAUTY IS ETERNAL AND LIVES LONG AFTER YOU GO

BE CERTAINLY CAREFUL OF THE SEED THAT YOU SOW

LIVE, LOVE, LEARN AND KEEP A SMILE ON YOUR LIPS

TOIL HARD AND NURTURE YOUR RELATIONSHIPS

SOW GOOD SEEDS IN THE RICH SOIL OF LIFE

CARVE OUT A GARDEN WHERE GOODNESS IS RIFE

KEEP TUNING AND REFINING YOUR CHARACTER

BECAUSE TRUE BEAUTY ALWAYS LAST FOREVER

Rejection

ENSNARED IN A TANGLED WEB OF DECEPTION
STABBED ONCE AGAIN BY THE KNIFE OF REJECTION
BLOOD OF ANGER GUSHED FROM WOUNDS OF HURT
I FLAILED AND WALLOWED IN EMOTIONAL DIRT
GARMENTS OF CYNICISM I WEAR AS A SHIELD
A SWORD OF SUSPICION NOW DEFENDS MY FIELD
MY HEART PADLOCKED IN THE DARK FAR AWAY
NEVER TO BASK IN THE SUNLIGHT OF DAY
OPTIMISM TURNED TO HOSTILE DISTRESS
SELF-DOUBT HAS BECOME MY IDEAL DRESS
MY SHOES OF TIMIDITY HAS MUD OF HATE
FOOD OF PESSIMISM I EAT FROM MY PLATE
FORGIVENESS I STORED AWAY ON A SHELF
A LOAD OF SELF-PITY I CARRY MYSELF
NOISE OF DEPRESSION KEEPS ME UP ALL NIGHT
REJECTION HAS STOLEN THE BITE FROM MY FIGHT
ONCE BITTEN AND TWO TIMES SHY
NOW FEAR GRIPS MY HEART, EVERY TIME I TRY

A Real Man

A REAL MAN SEES A WOMAN FOR MUCH MORE THAN HER PRETTY
FACE
HE LOOKS BEYOND HER MAKE-UP AND HER DRESS TO UN-LACE
HE IS LEAST CONCERNED WITH HER SCORE ON THE SCALE
OR HOW MUCH SHE EATS CURRY AND OXTAIL
SHE NEEDS NOT BE A MODEL ON THE PAGES OF VOGUE
OR DRESSES IN PRADA SHOES OR SCOTTISH BROGUE
HE FALLS IN LOVE WITH HER SOUL AND HUMBLE HEART
AND IS NOT INCLINED TO WALK AWAY WHEN THE DAYS GET DARK
HE COMMITS WITHOUT THE APPROVAL OF HIS FRIENDS
IS UNCOMPROMISING WHEN HIS HOUSEHOLD HE DEFENDS
UNFORTUNATELY WOMEN OFTEN PASS HIM BY
SINCE HE NOT INTO THE 'BLING' AND IS OFTEN SHY
HIS STRENGTH IS SEEN AS WEAKNESS TO THOSE OF
NARROWNESS
YET HIS QUALITIES ARE CRAVED IN TIMES OF DISTRESS
HIS TYPE SEEMS TO BE OUT OF STYLE
SINCE THE MASSES CRAVE THINGS CRAZY AND WILD
HE IS A GEM LOST IN THE DUST OF BRAND NAMES
NOT STRUTTING STARDOM OF EPHEMERAL FAME
OFTEN IT'S TOO LATE WHEN HE IS DISCOVERED
BY BATTERED HEARTS THAT LIFE HAS RETIRED

Disturbed

Tired of being constantly rudely disturbed

Pushed off the sidewalk, kicked to the curb

In the middle of a party the blaring sirens

Banging on the door, it's now a crime scene

Tired of people interrupting my thoughts

Car wheels screeching on the street I cross

Talking on the phone a beep on the line

Someone's always seeking to invade my time

Cut off often times in the middle of my speech

Some people just never know the right time to speak

Nice to have a decent conversation with the boss

Hope he allows me to get my point across

Lost in a dream somewhere sitting in a park

Startled by a puppy dog been taken for walk

Seems like one cannot get a peaceful break

Disturbance everywhere on every route you take

Yet life must go on despite my complaints

Peace of mind is a luxury enjoyed by the saints

Blue Monday

Hard to get out of bed this morning

Can't face the day

Fearing the vultures that's waiting

Mounting bills to pay

Yesterday's problems still clogs my mind

Enough on my plate

Tears of bad decisions making me blind

Can't escape my fate

Facing those who stand in judgement

The murderous pack

Tossed to and fro on waves of torment

Lashing my back

Resilience worn to the very last strand

Can't handle no more

Losing my footing on the ground I stand

Need options to explore

My feet of lead now refuse to move

Inertia takes its hold

Pushed to accept I've lost my grove

Less than being bold

Deadlines and obligations to meet

Noose around my neck

The shackles of circumstance bind my feet

Handed a shortened deck

Life's volcanic lips spewing its fire

Melting my core

Dreadful monstrous biting vampire

Ugly agonizing sore

Gaping, painful, indelible scar

Unbearable misery

Falling short of the shining star

Desiring the glory

First Casualty of War

Truth becomes the first

Among the casualties to fall

It is first to be besmirched

To justify a war

Facts become fictitious

To facilitate the vicious

The victor then with his pen

Records his pyrrhic gain

With fervent hate he perpetuates

The vanquished endless pain

He calls them bad and plants his flag

To occupy their space

Another day to stop and say

What a colossal waste

The script becomes a holy writ

Lives become the pawn

Families cry as dads say goodbye

To ride the desert storm

We can tell that war is hell

Even truth burns in a wink

Passing years drenched with tears

Truth will swim but never sink

If war must come when it's all said and done

Let truth be the cause

No one should fight and exploit

Just to earn man's applause

Share with a friend the spoils we spend

To mutilate and scar

Separate need from evil greed

And hush the noise of war

The unchecked cruel finds much fuel

In the pit of wicked lies

Innocent blood flows like a flood

As men drop dead like flies

Both the wicked and the timid

Have selective eyes

Truth is truthful; lies are useful

Either one can make you rise

One upgrades while one degrades

One is transient as the grass

One will let you win the battle

But only truth victory will last

Justice n Peace

Peace, peace, but at what cost

Whose peace will come at my loss

Peace for whom and peace for what,

Whose freedom and blood will pay for that

Who will scream and who will weep

Whose body will be going 6ft. deep?

Peace, peace, is high on your list

But who advocates for social justice

The blood of injustice paints the streets red

There's no hoopla when a poor man is dead

There are no vigils by dignitaries and kings

No one is preoccupied with ordinary things

Peace, peace, but how does it compute

Who gets hurt when they take aim and shoot

Who shake and tremble in coldness and chill

Who will be buried on top of Boot Hill

Whose tear drenched pillow is ever wet

Whose life dangles from the rope of neglect

Peace, peace, has no color or creed

The tree of corruption is watered by greed

Cover-ups and nepotism rules the day

The weak and downtrodden have to pay

The wheels of justice has no grease

Peace wilts and dwindles while wars increase

Religion

The peace we chase will not take place

As long as there's religion

From humans came, and kingdoms reign

It has always caused division

The Mormons say they are the way

And everything else is a farce

The Christians preach, their doctrines

teach

Outside of Christ your lost

The Muslims hold and expressed in bold

Allah is the only God

The Atheist claim, and makes it plain

To believe in the Divine is bad

The Gnostic clan elevates man

Proclaim him god of his exalted state

The Hindu dogma promotes karma

Making man the author of his fate

Wars have waged from age to age

Allegedly divinely mandated

God has fought deep in man's heart

So we've all been educated

Science have tried and sometimes lied

It too has become religious

We have been used and confused

While chaos reigns around us

Jesus came, proclaimed His name

Invited man to a relationship

Man's response and preferred stance

Is to create a complex religious kit

Instead of love from high above

Man seek for reason to be divisive

Judgement rains and man cast blames

Finding it hard to forgive

Some claim great might and espouse

moral light

Yet they fumble in blind darkness

The walls that divide rise high like a tide

Some are even disliked for their kindness

Women are fettered, scarred and battered

By the whip of religious convenience

Men so depraved seek to kill and enslave

Those with less than ideal experience

Many are zealous and extremely religious

Yet lacking in moral light

Basically mean and perversely extreme

Taking from others their rights

It's totally sad and more than just bad

Doing all of these things in God's name

Some think it's legit and refuse to admit

That such deplorable act is a shame

What more will it take to write on the slate

That we're all better off united

Death in the streets, some have nothing to eat

While the increase of religion is unabated

Technological advancement creates much excitement

Yet man's character declines

We are individualistic and downright selfish

Our best days are sadly behind

Like a growing virus the world gets more religious

And man grows more callous in his heart

A spate of injustice and malignant malice

Keeps friends and families apart

We wait for a change, a time to rearrange

The paradigm that has long failed us

We seek godliness and neighbourly respect

A people that are gentle and just

The answer my friend is not the cash you spend

But a realignment of man and his Maker

Things head to decay every night and day

Only spiritual things last forever

No need for offences, embrace differences

While keeping your own principles in place

No room for judgement; let's seize the moment

Aren't we all recipients of grace

Sometimes

Sometimes we have to lose it all to find back our way

Ripped apart and crumpled like a potter's melted clay

Dreams must be shattered to awake us from our daze

Our feet must sometimes dangle on edge of our graves

Sometimes we have to lose it all to find back our groove

Our feet need to be broken to remind us why we move

Our eyes need to be darkened so we value our sight

Our day needs to be stressful so we appreciate the night

Sometimes we have to lose it all to realize what we had

Looking back we will know, that it wasn't all that bad

We need some disappointments to stop us in our track

It's too easy to be complacent and overly relaxed

Sometimes we have to lose it all to value our health

Reminded of past scarcity to care for our wealth

We have to face the music once and for all

And let flying scattered chips lie where they fall

Sometimes we have to lose it all, to really know a friend

That's when you know who is real and those who pretend

The cream will rise to the top, just when it is right

And real will be the arms you feel in your darkest night

Sometimes you have lose it all to experience true gain

You have to swim against the tide; be beaten by the rain

You have to face your darkest fear once and for all

Marching at your enemy and rising from your fall

Significance

We live for it and we die for it
We strive for it and were born for it
We train for it and take risks for it
We pray for it and dearly pay for it
We love for it and hate for it
It's called, significance!

❖

It's the reason we for which we exist
Every man and nation needs a piece of it
Wars are waged in the name of it
Lies are told in the quest for it
Millions expended for the thrill of it
It's called, significance!

Religions exist for the cause of it
Science is pursued to get a hold of it
Everyone wants to experience it
Life means nothing if we don't have it
That's why so much blood is shed for it
It's called, significance!

❖

It's why we dream, aspire and prod
It drives countless souls to believe in God
It's the demand of the universe on
every heart
To find one's gift then play well the part
It's a cut above average and ordinary
It's called, significance!

If The Truth Be Told

If the truth be told who would really want to know?

Who wants to let go off a lie when the truth comes like a blow?

Who wants to know what really is, and what must come to pass?

Who wants to embrace the NOW at the risk of losing the familiar past?

Is there more truth in the darkness than what is in the light?

Who hungers for truth more than the need to always be right?

Is truth a convenience; a means to an end; a tool for expedient mechanism?

Is it absolute, relative, definitive, subjective, exclusive; a truism?

Whose truth is the truth, your truth, my truth, their truth or His truth?

Whose truth set us free, empowers, encourages, emboldens without being

aloof?

Whose truth advances the cause of every human being?

Whose truth works all things together for good for those who have faith in Him?

Whose truth has set my life on course?

Whose truth is responsible for the universal force?

Whose truth shall stand when all else fall?

Whose truth rings through in the fate of the Jericho walls?

Who shall seek this truth and drink from this cup that is often bitter?

Who will choose what is real; what is right; what is honourable; what is better?

X-Slave

I survived slavery through my fore-father's strength

I survived slavery through my ancestors' resilience

I survived slavery because my people were strong

I survived slavery because they stood against wrong

I survived been pushed overboard to die in the sea

I survived to be all that my people could not be

I survived slavery!

I survived choosing death over the slave master's whip

I survived jumping to freedom off his dark dirty ship

I survived the ten million who died being slaves

I survived as a living wreath of respect on their graves

I survived the hang man's brutal tree

I survived because my people die to make me free

I survived slavery!

I survived the attempts to destroy my language

I survived been treated like a vicious savage

I survived been sold and animalized

I survived been hated and demonized

I survived the distortion of my history

I survived to eat the sweet fruit of liberty

I survived slavery!

I survived because my people fought for this day

I survived because they did not forget to pray

I survived because many dangled from the rope

I survived because they kept alive the hope

I survived because of my ancestors' genetic pedigree

I survived to complete the journey started for me

I survived slavery!

I survived although they took away my name

I survived and have no need to be ashamed

I survived because no other people could

I survived because evil will never conquer good

I survived being evaluated as three fifth of human being

I survived a slave master who was wretched and mean

We survived slavery!

No Surrender

They were proud to be black and refused to be slaves

They fought with fierce vengeance and stood like a brave

They endured the long trek of the Trans-Atlantic

Though millions perished and never made it

Some escaped from plantations and took to the hills

Where they preserved their culture and sharpen their skills

Chanting and dancing in the light of the moon

A resilient proud people called the Maroons

Pursued like wild pigs by slave catcher attacks

They stood up with Cudjoe and beat them all back

Their weapons were simple, but they had intellect

It was death before dishonour or disrespect

The African ways they would never disown

Such rich cultures and savannahs to roam

So load up those muskets and sound the abeng

The freedom war is on, let's bring it to them

Call up the elders, says the warrior Nanny

No retreat, no surrender, no peace treaty

Cries for Justice

Kareen Farquharson

Somewhere out there on yonder hill
A savage hunts for more blood to spill
The cries go up for justice delayed
One more corrupt legislator is paid
Kids denied the pleasures of hobbies
Radiant dreams croak in limp lifeless
bodies
While grieving mothers bury their dead
Criminals sleep in suave feathered beds

So many children can't go out to play
And justice grew wings and flew away
O justice we search for your domicile
Without you we just cannot reconcile
We cry for your fairness and even-hand
To restore harmony and heal our land
Your wheels seem to take forever to turn
While villainous scoundrels loot and
burn

Words Kill

Sticks and stones can break my bones

But words are as fatal as military drones

Hurtful and harmful words copiously abound

Sly and suspicious words can easily be found

Mean and malicious words cut to the core

Virulent and vicious words make a sickening sore

Malignant and menacing words make you scream

Discouraging and demeaning words kill self-esteem

Bitter and berating words designed to keep you down

Offensive and odorous words make you wear a frown

Extreme and excessive words obscure true light

Contentious and combative words lead to a fight

Doubtful and dubious words undermine security

Scalding and sardonic words defame integrity

Spitting and spewing from defiled and dirty lips

Destroying and devastating sacred relationships

The piercing power of hurting words never is in doubt

Pays to listen and think before you tilt your spout

Fear Monster

Fear like crippling tightening wires
Paralyzing sands in my shoes of desires
The grit that stops the wheel of my will
The boulder that pulls me backward down hill
Gripping and blocking my every attempt
Aggressively sapping every ounce of my strength
Whispering lewd dirty lies in my ear
Hijacking my courage with gloomy despair
Raping my pride and making me naked
Taking from me that which is sacred
Derailing my train on the line of success
Spewing his smoke of pain and distress
Seizing me bleeding me making me weak
Putting his shackles of doubt on my feet
Taunting and haunting, pursuing my hide
Making a mockery of my honour and pride
Kicking and punching me into the dust
Draining the juice of my impetus
Mauling me stalling me tearing my flesh
Hunting and luring me into his mesh
Choking the neck of my resolve and grit
Fear is a monster that just never quits

Tropical Bliss

This was one time for sure I was gonna sit it out

Steep hills ahead were one too many and the sun blazed a shout

In the heart of the tropics time is meaningless

One never had to hurry so I sat down to rest

Can't recall a time she wasn't, and today she was there

I grew conscious of her fingers in my bushy Afro-hair

Bewitched and enchanted; she always hits the spot

Her persistent teasing had me sprawled on my back

What unfolded as I laid there arrested by her gaze

My senses were heightened; I melted in a daze

The coolness of her breathing; feathery smoothness of its touch

Her picturesque physique, had me in a mush

I basked in the melodies of her repertoire of voices

And breathed a prayer of thanks, to be honourably exploited

Birds chirped, grass rustled, mice scurried off to hide

Lizards croaked, dogs howled and a mule scratched its side

They all acquiesce to her decree —even me I dear say

I was there for her taking; would have it no other way

Tethered to the end of her string under her full control

She played me like a violin; mounted me like a pole

Riding high above the clouds and looking below

Never seen such fertile lands, where milk and honey flow

Swinging high from the ceiling, in a wild and lawless zone

Nothing lasts in dream-land; got to head on back home

Swooned just for a moment, I gently rubbed one eye

Must have been out for a while, by where the sun hanged in the sky

She was still there when I woke up, with my face wearing a smile

The hills beckoned and she nudged me; time for a homeward climb.

As a boy growing up my grandfather would send me to water his cows which were grazing quite a far distance from home. Most days the sun was so intolerably hot, that I would fall asleep under a big shaded mango tree and waited until the day was cooler before I started my uphill trek back home. This poem was inspired by the pleasant memories of those times when I was one with nature.

Lavanya

She was just a seedling one day
Slowly sprouted into to a flower
Learning bits and pieces on the way
Getting sweeter by the hour
Never is a fleeting moment
She does not evoke a smile
So un-defiled and innocent
The essence of a child
Her laughter rings with music
Her cries tell of her fears
She learns a word and uses it
The cutest clothes she wears
She is poetry in motion
A ballerina in her stance
So graceful in her action
Too alert to miss a chance
Her questions bring amazement
Seems she pluck them from thin air
Her soul proclaims endearment
Her giggles bring us cheer
She does a task and celebrates
Succeeds and beams with joy
Her dad she likes to imitate
And plays mom like a toy
Most precious in her baby world
Wrapped in garments of innocence
The gift of this little girl
A perfect pearl of excellence
Growing stronger and smarter
As the years go ticking by

Won't be long she's at the alter
And then tears will flood my eyes
So what are little girls made of
Can words paint a picture true
We can think of all the good stuff
She's a gift unwrapped each day anew

This poem is dedicated to my 6 year
old daughter Lavanya. It was written
when she was about 4 years old.

Bovrell G Simpson

Mama Hands

From the moment felt life, I was glued
to her hands
Hands that fed me, hands that steered
me as I traversed life's troubled land
Hands of care and courage; hands that
scrubbed my filthy clothes
Hands that touched me; hands that
soothed me: hands that wiped my
runny nose
Hands that laboured for long hours;
hands that never seemed to rest
Hands of love and blessings; hands
that gave of all their best
Hands that guided my footsteps;
hands that never spared the rod
Hands that nursed me back to
wellness; hands for which I'm very
glad
Hands that picked from the canvas
when tossed to wall
Hands that cradled me with comfort,
when I was bruised from a fall
Hands of strength and service; hands

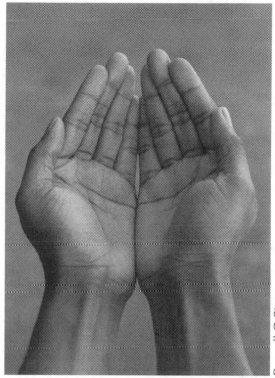

Bovrell G Simpson

that never idly hang
Hands that's always giving, bringing
joy to everyone
And when those hands moved no
more, I lost my biggest fan
You were always in my corner, gladly
cheering me along
Today your hands are still on me; you
have truly left your mark
I am missing you forever; keeping you
deep in my heart

East Indian

Went to see her today at
the place we first met
With my heart pounding
wildly against my chest
Once each year she visits
just about this time
And I melted like jello
when her alluring eyes
met mine
I had waited for many
months with desires of
my own
We must find a get-away
to spend some time alone
Trapped somewhere
deep in her succulent
skin
Was something so
sumptuous calling me in
My lips started shaking,
my heart somersaults
I just could not wait to
tear her apart
My body convulsed like a
meteorite shower
As I peeled back her skin
to bite into her flower
Overcome by the
eagerness to be set loose
My tongue in suspension
licks her sweet juice
This was much better
than when I met Julie
She was too wild and
downright unruly
The crunching grinding
of my teeth in her flesh
Drove me so crazy my
whole face was wet
Like a bull whose intent
is to crash the fair
My teeth got entangled
in her bushy long hair
Pulling each strand in
symphonic flow
Clenching my fist and
curling my toe
Licking and moaning for
what I long craved
No problem being buried
like this in my grave
Her sweetness burns
and dilates my vein
Copiously refreshing
like tropical rain
Proudly I lift my full
glass in toast
Of all my desires I crave
her the most
The smile on my face
when it's all done
Tells her precisely the
depth of my fun
While I wait expectantly
to taste her again
I lust for her sweetness
from now until then
I love and adore her and
compare her to no one
My succulent, gorgeous,
and juicy East Indian

This poem is about my love affair with a type of mango that is commonly known as "East Indian," in Jamaica and other parts of the Caribbean. Another type of mango referenced in this poem, is called "Julie."

Bovrell G Simpson

Frenemies

Their unspoken words like leprosy
Eats your flesh voraciously
The venom from their nasty threats
Their rotten wishes and viciousness
Their thoughts like spiders many legs
Spin sly deceptive wicked webs
Their insatiable ravenous appetite
Like a million sucking parasites
Their silent eyes like dirty fingers
Rove your body with chilling lingers
Their hands so cold, clammy and damp
Unwilling extended clumsy clamp
Their eyes bulging with bitter hate
They dump toxic poison on your plate
You must be shrewd to elude
Don't even think to eat their food

It

The good old days are not coming back, get over it
Life is not a game you play, get real with it
Your wife is not your mother, get use to it
You're not entitled to anything, go work for it
Your marriage is not a wedding, so adjust to it
Youth doesn't last forever, so make the best of it
Your fate is in your hands, so take care of it
Not everyone will agree with you, so roll with it

❖

If time is not enough, your complaint is wasting it
If you fail, don't blame the world for it
If no one is helping, please get on with it
If you have a problem, you should be solving it
If life is not kind to you, start being kind to it
If it's your mistake, you should lay claim to it
If you break the law prepare to pay for it
If you wake up the lion, prepare to fight with it

❖

When in doubt question it
When conviction comes believe in it
When you fail, learn from it
When the tide is high, rise with it
When the flow is good go with it
When the rhythm is nice bounce to it
When the funds are low live with it
When the time is bad be good to it

❖

Because whether you live or die with it
Climb the hill or swim the sea for it
Search the world or advertise for it
Organize or negotiate for it
Get it free or pay a lot for it
Ignore or be obsessed with it
Laugh or gallivant with it
We are altogether stuck with it!

Tropical Repose

Grandpa said to me one day

The cows need water and fresh hay

Down miles of dusty hills I trekked

Donned floppy hat and water bucket

The cows were pleased to see my face

Fresh green grass and water to taste

Cows were fed; copiously refreshed

Duties completed, my list was checked

The sun's sharp sword was merciless

Piercing my skin draining my sweat

Steep hills ahead melted from heat

Big shaded tree was a welcome retreat

Needed the rest to embark on the task

Instantaneously fell asleep in the grass

Cradled in nature's arms so serene

Peaceful in slumber, lost in a dream

Oblivious to reality, remotely detached

Tropical repose, anywhere unmatched

Lingered for respite in midday paradise

Feathery breeze as cooling as ice

Until time dulled the sun's sharp edge

Tarried in slumber in a king straw bed

Certainly could do it all over again

Living the life of story book children

Looking to those times sleeping in the

grass

A luxury for many that comes at a cost

Re-tracing steps through the trail of

the mind

A futile attempt to turn back the

time . . . .

Sometimes

Sometimes you must take a stand although it is painful
Sometimes you have to tell the truth although it is hurtful
Sometimes you must hold your tongue for a peaceful life
Sometimes you must be firm even if it causes strife
Sometimes you must to be silent in order to look smart
Sometimes you must ignore your brain and listen to your heart
Sometimes you must believe yourself without having to explain
Sometimes you have to cry at jokes and laugh at your pain
Sometimes you have to love some friends from a distant far
Sometimes you have to hitch your wagon to a flying star
Sometimes you must be content with whatever is at hand
Sometimes you have to crawl around before you get to stand
Sometimes you have to sigh because you have no words
Sometimes you have to break away from the running herd
Sometimes you have to fake it until you can make it
Sometimes it is shameful but you just have to admit
Sometimes it is harmful but we still persist
Sometimes it is okay to cross names from your list
Sometimes it is good to delete numbers from your phone
Sometimes it is good to do some things alone
Sometimes it is not necessary to do some things sometimes
Sometimes sometime is not the best of the times
Sometimes it's just the right time for sometimes
Sometimes sometime is just sublime sometimes

Moon Lover

Last night the moon and I went on a date

Our nocturnal escapade went on until late

Everything unfolded like we were in a dream

She was certainly the best topping on my cream

The paint-brush of her silver light touched every tree

And she set aside the night to shine for only me

Her light of dainty fingers traced my glowing skin

Her overwhelming presence caused my head to spin

I was lost in her bosom of intoxicating calm

My eyes roved each line of her mystic palm

Her kisses lit my body from my head to my toe

Her sparkling eyes were gravid with alluring glow

She led me like a prized horse from its cozy stall

Toward the regal crystal room just beyond a hall

What I saw there was just exquisitely serene

I was speechless in amazement at this magical scene

I can tell you this much, not a single word more

She is a wave I'd always like to wash upon my shore

I wish she comes to get me when my nights are blue

If you're lucky sometimes she will also come for you

Bovrell G Simpson

The "F" Word

We all have used the 'F' word in our life along the way

Some have used it with such gusto that would blow you out the way

It takes guts to use the 'F' word, which brings powerful relief

Never use it when you're upset, it's more effective when at ease

They ought to teach the 'F' word in all of our schools

It's an essential commodity among life's greatest tools

Jesus used the 'F' word, and He was very kool

He implores us to use it, so don't be disobeying fools

The "F" word is cathartic; it is good for the heart

When your foe earns it, let him have it full blast

Stand up on the hilltop, and let everyone hear

Let them stand and marvel, as the mighty "F" word blares

Every "F" word user should be proud and not be shy

If a preacher does not use it, he is telling you a lie

O if we all would use the 'F' word, what a fruitful life we'd live

Countless are the wondrous blessings, if we just learn to FORGIVE

Forgiveness is that 'F' word that relieves much of life's pain

I forgive you for thinking, I was blaspheming Jesus name

The Sun Came Out Today

The sun came out again today
I'm glad it did not stay away
It's rays danced on my windowsill
Like a super energy boosting pill
It fills me up with life anew
There's so much that I want to do
I want to climb a mongo tree
Walk about the place carefree
Set free from the master clock
Enjoy the hammock where I rock
I want to talk with old man Joe
He has so much I want to know
Then I must see my old aunt Sue
She has chores I can help do
I can help to clean her tiny house
Watch her big cat chase a mouse
I want to play some dominoes
Dance quadrille and heel and toes
I want to hang out with my friend
Jakey
He drinks a bit but he's not crazy
I want to feel that jolly mood
Friends and I go cook some food

I want to play tennis ball cricket
Bowl quick deliveries to hit the wicket
Watch the girls play Chinese skip
Hear sweet laughter from their lips
I want to lay down in the grass
Count the birds that's flying pass
Walk barefoot in water puddles
Catch butterflies and blow bubbles
I want to sit and laugh and talk
Take nice Sunday evening walks
I want to leap, shout and yell
Listen to stories grandma tell
I want to eat bammy and steam fish
Drink red peas soup from my dish
And when the sun is about to set
Paints red the sky and then plummet
I want to sit in the evening shade
Sip some tea that is homemade
And when I finally close my eyes
I'll set my mind on the next sunrise

I Am Pregnant

Today I leap out of bed
Feeling lively and jubilant
A peculiar feeling through me spread
Alas! I am pregnant
❖
I am pregnant it shows
Every sign can tell
Exuding the most happy glow
My appetite swells
❖
I am pregnant with optimism
Chomping at the bit
Have a rush of altruism
Hard to stand still or sit
❖
I am pregnant with love
Filling me right up
The Man from above
Brewed me a cup
❖
I am pregnant with music
Have to get it out
A human acoustic
Makes me sing and shout

❖
I am pregnant with kindness
To spread joy around
Sharing sacred sweetness
Of generosity I found
❖
I am pregnant with hope
It's a great outlook
Scanning a panoramic scope
Etched my name in life's big book
❖
I am pregnant with praise
For the Most High
My voice shall I raise
And bid my spirit fly
❖
I am pregnant with passion
A strong live wire
The heat of emotion
Like a red volcanic fire
❖
I am pregnant and will give birth
My water has broken
I'll spread my offspring all over Earth
Please accept my token

Mother Nature

Let us with healthy pleasure
Enjoy bounties of the earth
Drink from the breast of Mother
Nature
The milk of new birth
Let us kiss with gaping lips
Her cheeks of strawberries
Eat from her fertile hips
The ripeness of her berries
Of fruits and trees
All full and ripe
Of honey making bees
Working day and night
So pristinely furnished
Nature brings pure health
Naturally embellished

A repository of wealth
From her womb of blessings
Mankind is replenished
A much needed refreshing
Without which we all would perish
Let us with open arms
Hug her with grateful attitude
Look on her unfolding charms
She's deserving of our gratitude
And amidst being abused
By men for filthy lucre
She still has not refused
To be a caring Mother

The Leaf that Fell

A leaf fell from a tree today
Gently swaying in the breeze
Glided smoothly on its way
To join other fallen leaves
I looked up just for a spell
To consider what I saw
Beheld the tree from which it fell
And pondered in great awe
It did not shed a weeping tear
For the leaf there on the ground
There were no signs of wear and tear
Nor a glum grieving frown
I wondered curiously
How this could really be
And marvelled at the mystery
Of this intriguing tree
Perhaps the leaf that fell
Was resting there at ease
Having done its duty well
And retired in placid peace
I considered the lesson
That unfurled before my eyes
And thought of many persons
And how they live their lives

One day just like that leaf
Our time will surely come
Leaving behind those filled with grief
When our work here is done
But like that leaf I must suggest
We do our duty well
Giving nothing but the best
Seeking always to excel
Then those who we leave behind
Will grieve but not in shame
Our deeds will stand the test of time
And our names grow wings of fame

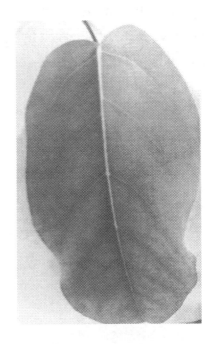

The Last Sunset

I waited for the sunrise this morning
But the clouds got in the way
The red horizon was sadly missing
With no sun to warm my day
No light to bounce silver rays
From the dew drenched grass
No heat to warm the coarse dry hay
Whose youthful time had passed
It occurred to me that yesterday
Was someone's last sunset
Last night he died where he lay
With life's painful regrets
He left a pile of things undone
And places to explore
Now he walks death's hall alone
Behind a cold dark door
Since today could be your last
You should make it counts
Live it well, have a blast
Cast out all fears and doubts
Share some joy and cheer a friend
Go and spread some peace
Forgive those who offend
Save your conscience from being obese

Bovrell G Simpson

Missed You Last Night

Last night I woke up crying
Because you were not home
The place that I was laying
Was cold and all alone
From the night of our wedding
You've kept me cozy and warm
But last night you were missing
From my warm and yearning arms
Now don't say I am feeble
You are my every-thing
I can soar just like an eagle
Because you're my darling
I could not wait for morning
When you would be back home
You're the master piece I'm missing
My sweetest honeycomb
You're the reason I'm still breathing
The cause for which I live
The light bulb in my ceiling
To you my all I give
Hurry home my Angel
Come on home my juice
Cast on me your love spell
That, I won't refuse
Please ring my doorbell
Say honey I am here
To put it in a nutshell
I am missing my dear

Bovrell G Simpson

90

Religion Not Christianity

When programs reign supreme above people
And practices are promoted above principle
When works pave the road to eternal bliss
And we pick and choose those we assist
When grace and mercy have lost their worth
And we strive for heaven based on works
When it is a sin to dress-up pretty
That is religion, not Christianity

When a woman is judged by the ring in her ear
And much is debated about the style of her hair
When righteousness is gained by the food you eat
Yet nothing is done for the poor in the street
When more attention is paid to the list of don'ts
And a failure to do the good things that we won't
When salvation depends on your gift of prophesy
That is religion, not Christianity

When praying to God requires linguistic correctness
And heaven is for those with self-earned righteousness
When education decides where you attend for church
And in times of need you are shunned and shirked
When living by faith is no longer in vogue
And the Holy Day becomes an enormous load
When men cast judgments without much pity
That is religion, not Christianity

When little care is shown to those within
Yet we rally the troops for evangelism
When influence is decided by the size of the tithe
And we trample the teachings of Jesus Christ
When style trumps the substantive essence of His word
And the church is led by spiritual nerds
When the thief and the preacher runs the city
That is religion, not Christianity

❖

When the voice of the poor is stifled and crushed
And their shepherds are terribly way out of touch
When the saints of the church are so polarized
And leaders are way above being criticized
When morality is decided by casting a vote
And the weak ones are thrown outside of the boat
When bureaucracy gets in the way of charity
That is religion, not Christianity

God Has No Needs

God has no needs or ego to feed
That's not the reason His laws you should heed
He does not need your praise or worship
That's not why He asked you to do it
God does not need a Sabbath in a seven day week
He made it for us as a special time to meet
There is nothing you can do to make Him more God
His perfection is immutably ironclad
Your actions cannot make Him less than perfect
Despite your rebellion and gross disrespect
God is not vain or insecure
That's why He gave you the choice to explore
At the risk of having you rebel against Him
He gave you the choice if you choose to sin
He puts man's destiny in his own hand
And bought insurance with salvation's plan
Be certain that whatever He asks you to do
Is solely intended to benefit you
He commands you to adhere to His laws
Which were designed to expose your flaws
If we all love our neighbors as we should
No crime would be in our neighborhood
Families would be intact if we did not divorce
We would be spared much grief and remorse

If we honor God with all our heart
Man would love light and shuns the dark
How does God benefit when obedience we employ
Except the satisfaction to see us brimming with joy
So whether we give or withhold obedience
It does not take away from God's divine essence
He is self-sufficient and will always be sovereign
But we have all to lose if we do not obey Him
So when you see God's laws don't resist and argue
It's the prescription of what God wants to do through you
It is in our best interest for eternal life
And obedience always supersedes sacrifice

Getting out of Bed

When the night and the morning intersect
And my body is screaming for some more rest
Sleep pulls me left and duty pulls me right
I pray to the Lord it was still night
My brain barks orders my eyes disobey
The clock on the wall keeps ticking away
Suspended somewhere between life and death
Cursing my luck, growing mad and upset
Someone please silence that crowing cock
And take a sledge hammer to that alarm clock
Hoping it could be another snow storm day
I would not have to work to get my pay
Delaying the inevitable of ditching the bed
My feet try to move but are as heavy as lead
Hard to abandon a blanket so cozy
To face a world so demanding and crazy
If I could just get a bit more sleep
Even if it is not that deep
Just to remove the jagged edge
The cloud that has formed inside my head
If I could turn off the sound in my ear
Ignore the voices of reason I hear
Curl up and snuggle in a sleeping bubble
Leaving the day alone with its trouble
Sleep till I hear a voice say sleep no more
Putting a no disturb sign on my door
But since there's job for which I was hired
And I dread to hear the words you are fired
I'll gather myself with all I can muster
And defy the lure of this bed pulling me closer

The Suffering Lamb

Who would die to save a perverse nation

Berated and banished; teased and spat upon

To think of the splendour, that he left behind

To suffer that agony for your sin and mine

Behold the dire sight through your mind's eye

They hunt him like a criminal, as if he feared to die

They took Him to Herod, and abuse at Him they hurled

They teased and ridicule Him, yet He never said a word

So they swap Him for Barabbas, a renowned culprit

Away with Him they shouted, to the bottomless pit

They beat him with whips that dug into His flesh

Such intense cruelty for our burdensome debt

It gave them pleasure to drive those cruel nails

And laughed as in anguish, He wrench from pain and wailed

Then that thief beside Him taunted, "Why don't you set us free,"

While his companion in compassion pleaded, "Lord, remember me."

When the soldiers pierced His side, agonizing pain rang through

He said, "Father forgive them, for they know not what they do."

His final words reverberate like a thunder in the sky

"Father, into thy hands I commit my spirit," and with those words He died

This man is amazing to have undergone all this

So that I could have a sure hope of eternal bliss

What a price to have paid for sinful mortal man

I just can't help, but to adore the Suffering Lamb

Saving Grace

I may never fully grasp
The richness of God's grace
So pristine in its holy task
Saving Adam's falling race

It embraces me in fullness
What-ever my sins are
Like a citadel or fortress
Surrounds me like a wall

Some say it is enabling
Of carnal pursuits
But I say it is forgiving
Equips me to bear good fruits

Grace supports my limitations
To live above the fray
In the darkness of transgression
It lights the only way

Grace comes at a high price
Paid by a loving God
His atoning sacrifice
Was His approving nod

If you drink the juice of grace
Do not drive the car of sin
Seize the chance to re-run the race
The greatest gift from Him

Justified

I am Barabbas
A decrepit crook
They swapped me for Jesus
On the cross my death He took
While I was the sinner
It was He who faced the mob
Now reprobates and liars
Saved from the wrath of God
Becoming what He was not
Imputing righteousness to me
Pulled me from the boiling pot
Fed me bread of liberty
Never more can I be lost
By a single sinful act
Fully paid for at the cross
A simple sacred fact
Accepting me as righteous
No merit to submit
His blood purifies us
Most holy and legit

Once vilified now justified
Once loss but now saved
Once hopelessly terrified
Now standing up in grace
He fired the old school master
Rendered him obsolete
I believe and surrender
Chains of works fell off my feet
Free from man's traditions
Of religious chores
With no power of redemption
Such a burdensome bore
With one last breath
He compensate
He silenced death
And sealed my fate
From the grave of bondage
He rose in victory
Taking death a hostage
Seized it for eternity

Destiny

If destiny's hand controls life's events

An end imposed without my consent

The unseen hand, which determines my end

The un-chosen choice I am left to contend

The foregone conclusion that must just be

The cup I must sip though I disagree

If I do not control who I shall become

Why should I pay for the wrongs I have done

Who pre-ordained one child to become a thief

A killer spreading mayhem and grief

A despot that rules with an iron fist

A swindler, a charlatan and a con artist

Who assigned poverty to be one man's fate

While to another is given all things great

If my decisions are not building blocks

The wind that determines where my ship docks

If the fate of my life is already sealed

Making me a bystander and not part of the deal

If my choices are inconsequential in the mix

And my nine is constantly been changed to a six

Should I then be judged condemned or punished?

The Voice

The voice in me, the voice in you
Telling us every day what to do
We hear it speaking everyday
Each one decides to choose a way
With ears to hear and the will act
The right to choose this way or that
We often choose to turn our ear
But the voice inside is always there
He allows you to contend and argue
And let you weigh the cardinal value
He convicts you when you run amok
And warns you not to push your luck
He is the ever present witness
Urging you to concede and confess
He tows that narrow moral line
And says what's yours and what is mine
He never shouts whenever he speaks
But surely stands on sturdy feet
He points out the strait and narrow
And accedes to your choice of sorrow
He will prompt without compelling
Leaving us to do the choosing
So when we play the ignorant game
The voice inside can't get the blame
Since we must live with choices we make
It behoves us to seriously deliberate
That voice in you and that in me
Is a powerful universal plea
It's the voice of God speaking to man
Making us according to His plan

Let's Get Drunk

If love is a potent wine
That binds the hearts of friends
Let's get drunk from her fertile vine
To a union that has no end
❖

Let's linger in her stupor
Get wasted senselessly
Like a consuming fire
Let love burns intensely
❖

Pour her in the glass of friendship
Let her chill on ice
Twirl her around before you sip
From the cheese of laughter take a slice
❖

Let's drink of love's sweet wine
Her wonders let's lament
Spread her in the sunshine
Watch her simmer and ferment
❖

Fill the glass of your heart
Way up to the brim
Spread your waiting lips apart
Be alive with her vigor and vim
❖

Let's guzzle down love's booze
Linger in her bar
Hatred feelings we must lose
And heal a hurtful scar
❖

For if we all get intoxicated
Throwing up gulps of love
Our world would be regenerated
Restored from up above

He Left

Today a husband left his wife
To settle for a tramp
They were married most of his life
Back then he was her champ
He left for what he claimed
Was real exotic taste
Everything went up in flames
When he found it was a waste
That thing of distant glitter
Was certainly not gold
It was a gall so bitter
His happiness was sold
The neighbour's grass was never greener
Distance created an illusion
If he had looked a little closer
He'd cherished his prized possession
Just an ounce of prevention
Would have done him more
Than to face this devastation
With no forthcoming cure
The bridge he burned behind
Sends up smoke of woe
Realizing he was blind
Wished he knew what he now knows
The rose petals that he crushed
Will live to once more bloom
Its leaves will once again be lush
But it won't grow in his room

She Left

Last month a woman left her man
To settle for a boy
They were married for so long
She was his pride and joy
She left for what she thought
Was love beyond belief
But things quickly fell apart
Now her heart is filled with grief
The boy she thought was so cute
A red hot fire coal
Turned out to be a wicked brute
With just one single goal
He was the classic cheater
Who never settled down
Known as a female beater
By every girl in town
The glitter she thought was gold
Was not even brass
She bought the phony she was sold
Made herself a big jackass
Hands she thought would hold her tight
And make her feel secure
Inflicted pain in bloody fights
And made her feel unsure
Now she's filled with regrets
Wished she never dumped her man
He was broken when she left
Now he has found someone

Perfection

Excuse me but I must insist

You drop me from your sinless list

For I have never made that claim

I don't play the perfect game

From your castle of faultless illusion

You exceed your personal jurisdiction

Unrelentingly you refuse to budge

A vaunted self-appointed judge

I have had my ups and downs

Fight demons and watch clowns

I have observed as life unfurled

Booted from your sinless world

I have countless places I must go

And lots of ways I have to grow

I have never claimed perfection

That is for the new creation

I endure the daily strife

It gives meaning to this life

I meekly embrace my fallibility

Seeking cure for my malady

So while you revel in your perfection

I will work out my own salvation

At the Potter's House

I went to potters house today
To watch him as he mould his clay
I took a seat upon the floor
To watch this long and tedious chore
He took the clay into his hand
And proceeded to work his plan
Spinning it slowly on his wheel
Holding on with hands of steel
Dissatisfied with what he saw
He crushed the clay to fix his flaw
He dictated what the clay became
To fit the image in his brain
I observed his power on exhibit
The creative rights to his credit
And then I thought of God above
So sovereign yet so full of love
We are just clay in His hand
A piece of the puzzle of His plan

In Him creative rights reside
Yet He allows us to decide
With just one word or a thought
The life we have could come to naught
The breath we breathe can be eclipsed
Our lifeless form down six foot six
And so I bowed in circumspect
To show some due divine respect
Because I am just a piece of clay
I don't even own the words I say
I drink from the cup of humility
Submit my will to God Almighty
And If He choose to break me now
In deep contrition I'll humbly bow
Let Him mould me as He may
Ever in His own sweet way

Kareen Farquharson

105

Fun-less Faith

If faith without its work is dead
Faith without fun is awfully dread
For what good would be faith's work
If fun was buried in dogmatic dirt
Constrained by the terror of transgression
Many are living in deep depression
Rejecting even to feel elated
Spiritually starved and constipated
Carrying around a Do Not list
Without a list of Do's to balance it
Paralysed by sterile polarizing religions
Spiritual rigor mortis and myopic visions
Telling everyone what they cannot do
Peddling doctrines that are not true
Feeding the people a diet of opinions
Sowing falsehood and wholesale confusion
Faith is freedom to embrace and celebrate
The boldness of love that conquers hate
Faith frees us from political correctness
Elevates people above bureaucratic process
Faith cuts the shackles of uniformity
Unites us amidst the throng of diversity
Faith prevails where reason has failed
It enters beyond that which was veiled
Faith takes away the mask from your face
Makes you stand in the fullness of grace
Faith must be more than what you can't do
An ocean of things fulfilling and true
Fun-less faith is something to shun
Yet we should not embrace faithless fun

The Poor are Rich

The poor are rich in kindness
Sharing the mite they hold
Wearing pearls of meekness
Around their hearts of gold

The poor are rich in courage
To hold on for dear life
Creatively they manage
To mount the hills of strife

The poor are rich beauty
Perfectly adorned
They dress in it neatly
Singing through the storm

The poor are rich in lessons
Of doing much with little
Changing one into a dozen
Make a fountain from a trickle

The poor are rich sorrow
Which they face each day
Yet they sing like a sparrow
On fallen knees they pray

The poor are rich in peace
To boldly face the night
Never getting an increase
But still putting up a fight

Abused Soul

Trapped soul in a vicious cycle
Smile of disguise hides her bruise
Emotional skin scarred and wrinkled
Taken, mauled and violently used

Helplessly drawn to her abuser
Weak, shattered self-esteem
Effortlessly yields to the loser
Selling her freedom, trading her dreams

Despoiled, cheapened, misused
Jaded and violently broken
Years of ill-treatment and abuse
Pride trampled and stolen

Ugly thoughts and feelings
Anaemic self image
Shattered heart that's bleeding
Nursing wounds of damage

❖

A world forever changed
Sadistic and cruel
Minds warped and deranged
Desperation her only fuel

Eyes on the horizon of hope
Scouting for redemption
Imbibing her daily dope
Of distress and disillusion

Searching for things long lost
Things she never had
Losing herself at all cost
A friend, a hero, a dad

Misunderstood and labelled
In a whirlpool of mess
Needing to be hugged and cradled
Freedom from this cycle of distress

Curiosity

Curiosity did not kill the cat
That laid there on the mat
It was not her quest to know
That unceremoniously ended her
show
She touched curiosity's flame
Possessing no reasoning acclaim
With no ability to moderate
It failed to win the hand of fate
Curiosity we should not blame
As a monster to hunt and tame
If curiosity is only a vice
Then so too is the gift of choice
Both tools can be misused
Over inflated and abused
If curiosity is just bad
Not an emotion made by God
Then children would never grow
They would not desire to know
Man would not experiment
Or explore his environment
We would not have the automobile
Or the invention of bricks and steel
We would never have paper
The cell phone or computer
Life would not be interesting
Without the desire for learning
We would not need schools

As we would be blissful fools
We could not do an MRI
Or fly a plane across the sky
We would not have subways
And nice expansive highways
We would not be romantic
Just boring and pedantic
We would not wonder who made us
Since we would not be curios
The reason why we grow
Is because we strive to know
When applied the way it should
Curiosity is very good
For even those who vilify
They are also asking why
While they curse the living fish
They eat it greedily from the dish
Yet they relegate this useful tool
Of themselves they make a fool
They too for knowledge yearn
Yet curiosity's bridge they burn
So if curiosity has killed your cat
Curiosity might just bring her back

Relic of Westminster

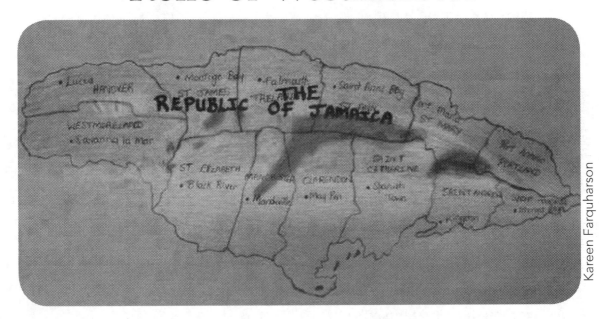

Kareen Farquharson

From the ashes of slavery a system immerged
The slave master's trick to keep us submerged
Bequeathing the Westminster model to his clones
The house slaves who now role from his throne
A system of power that accounts to no one
An elective dictatorship, oppressive and wrong
Led by a chief of one of the tribes
They juggle balls of rhetoric and marbles of bribes
Politicians pursuing their own selfish need
Clothed in corruption and garments of greed
Peddling deceptions, and trafficking treachery

With bulging bellies of greed and gluttony
While the suffering poor gets no reprieve
They manufacture schemes to divide and deceive
With MP's as proxies doing their bidding
The people's agenda is glaringly missing
While we hunger and languish in hopeless dirt
Our leaders stoutly put politics first
They jostle at trough of political spoils
Taxing the people who slavishly toil
They make policies for electoral expedience
While we pay the cost for their fiscal imprudence
They look through eyes of myopic vision
Mired in rituals of empty religion
They govern by making grand announcements
Blaming the next tribe for the lack of achievements
By every means they procure their fun
By the bible, the ballot, the bullet or the gun
With ideas so crude and sinister
They follow their god of Westminster
Their policies are like pyramid schemes
With political rhetoric and catchy themes
Acting without conscience or bridle
Policies are planned around electoral cycle
Using tribalism to divide the sheep
Killing each other for spoils of deceit
They worship the Head and adore the Bell
Prostitute their rights while living in hell
Trapped in a cycle stifling and tragic
Enslaved in a system of colonial relic

Alternating between tribes at the polls
For painful suffering and high death toll
Growing deficit and mounting debt
Like dangling noose placed around our neck
And each time the bucket bottom falls out
The people provide another bail-out
We crave for things to be rearranged
But under this system nothing will change
We need a leader the people directly elect
Not a dictator chairing a quasi cabinet
Give us a president voted by the electorate
Not a leader who answers to party delegates
We need MP's representing their constituents
Not party faithful with political intents
Give us representatives obligated to the people
Not political quacks or tribal disciples
We need a Republic of the Jamaican people
Based on our indigenous values and principles
Let the people's voice dictate our path
After fifty yours of achieving nought
This society must be transformed
Let's get our constitution reformed
We need a system where corruption can't flourish
But the old order must first be abolished
We deserve something substantially better
Than a manipulable system of Westminster
Give us something fair and accountable
Something superior to the Westminster model

Bio

Laval Wilkinson is a Child and Youth Counsellor, teacher, poet, fledging author, and freelance writer. He is a native son of Jamaica who resides in Ontario, Canada with his wife TracyAnn and daughter Lavanya. He currently works as a Child and Youth Counsellor in the classroom, where he counsels children and youth with emotional and behavioural problems. He is also the Program Co-ordinator for Cavalry Child and Family Services.

Laval is an avid reader and has been writing poems for over twenty years. He worked as a teacher with the Ministry of Education in Jamaica, before he moved to Canada in 2001. He taught for one year in Toronto, Canada before he became a Child and Youth Counsellor. In a three year hiatus from the classroom, Laval worked as a Client Services Manager for a marketing company in Toronto, before going back to his passion, working with children and youth. His absence from Jamaica is hardly noticeable as he has immersed himself in charitable work there assisting the poor and less fortunate, the very roots from which he comes. He contributes to public discourses through the publication of letters in the two major newspapers on the island. He is passionate about his country of birth, and has a deep interest in the political and socio-economic condition of his native home.

Over the years Laval has used the medium of poetry, and writing in general, to share his views and perspectives on life. As one who grew up in abject poverty, and did not attend high school, yet qualified himself to pursue tertiary education, he is an unrepentant believer in converting stumbling blocks into stepping stones. He has found his voice in writing, which he has utilized to share his enthusiasm for life and optimistic outlook.